THE CREDIT GAME

PLAYS WE WERE NEVER TAUGHT

CHEVON K. PATRICK

DISCLAIMER

This book is presented solely for educational purposes. The author and publisher are not offering it as legal or financial planning services advice. Every individual situation is different, and the advice and strategies contained herein may not be suitable for your situation.

While best efforts have been used in preparing this book, the author and publisher make no representations or warranties of any kind and assume no liabilities of any kind with respect to the accuracy or completeness of the contents and specifically disclaim any implied warranties of merchantability or fitness of use for a particular purpose.

Neither the author nor the publisher shall be held liable or responsible to any person or entity with respect to any loss or incidental or consequential damages caused, or alleged to have been caused, directly or indirectly, by the information or programs contained herein. No warranty may be created or extended by sales representatives or written sales materials.

CONTENTS

I dedicate this book to those who wish to empower themselves and others. America's wealth gap has been made worse by an education gap—a gap between the financial education given to the children of the rich vs. the children of the middle and working classes.

Many of us were never taught about credit or financial literacy. I know how easily this can lead to disaster, and feelings of helplessness and hopelessness. It doesn't have to be that way. We can all learn how to use the credit and financial systems we are born into to our advantage and build wealth for our communities.

This book is written to help you to accomplish just that.

CHAPTER 1
THE CREDIT TRAP

THERE WAS a time when I knew nothing about credit. Like so many people, I knew that credit cards appeared to be free money, and frankly couldn't care less about what happened to my unpaid bills. With credit, I could spend money I did not actually have and unpaid debts afforded me more money on hand.

As a young teen mother struggling to survive, I could have access to experiences and material things that my minimum wage income did not allow for. Credit cards and spending beyond my means could give me a glimpse of a better life.

Most everybody I knew used credit cards this way: as a lifeline to a better future they would someday catch up to. I planned to pay my debts back *someday*.

But maybe my plan to pay them back wasn't as solid as I thought. And maybe, in the midst of being offered more and more free money, I lost track of how much I actually owed.

What was the worst that could happen? And an even better question, how come we weren't taught about credit in school?

I didn't know what my credit score was, and no one I knew ever mentioned credit. It was one of those things that we heard people talking about on TV, but which never actually became relevant in our lives.

Later, I would learn the long history of government policies that facilitated wealth for white Americans and not blacks. If we'd known more about credit and finance, we might not have felt the need to borrow money we could not repay. We might have actually *had* that life of ownership and wealth that we spent our time and credit dreaming of.

I had saved up enough money to start college, and borrowed several thousands more to pay the ongoing costs of tuition. I'd gotten good grades, following the pre-Recession wisdom of getting the most prestigious education I could under the assumption that this would pay massive financial dividends. Unfortunately, I also had the Recession to worry about. Like so many people, I found that the degree I had paid so much for did not pay me back as much as I'd been promised.

After graduation, I was in trouble. I had finally discovered the truth about credit scores at the worst possible time. The truth was, if you had a bad credit score, you could find yourself out on the street.

Landlords were running credit checks, and turning me down for housing when they saw my frightening credit score. I couldn't buy or rent a car without paying extortionary double-digit interest rates and heavy down payments because of my poor credit. I was even denied a promising job after a would-be employer ran a credit check and decided that my irresponsible financial history would make me a liability to their company.

These past years, as I'd been using alternative methods like dead end jobs, selling drugs, financial aid, government assistance, and credit cards to survive motherhood and college, I had borrowed money without paying it back. Now I was being told that I *couldn't* pay it back, because I was being denied employment and forced to take ultra-high-interest loans which cost far more than paying out of pocket with cash would have cost me.

This is the trap of poverty: it is *expensive* to be poor. Everything costs more when you can only afford to buy a little at a time. Everything costs more when you have to agree to high-interest loans instead of paying with cash or a good line of credit.

And this is the trap of credit cards: they *want* to lend you money, because they want to charge you interest and late fees. But the credit trap is one you can use to your advantage.

Credit card companies and credit bureaus must perform a delicate dance to stay in business. They must convince people to borrow money from them so that they can make money on interest and late fees. But they must also ensure that *most* people pay that money back, so that they don't take a huge net loss.

This is where our complicated credit system comes in. The financial system *wants* you to borrow money. But it only wants you to borrow what you can pay back soon. It rewards you for behaving this way: when you borrow money and then pay it back almost immediately, your credit score goes up. And the higher your credit score, the less interest you are charged on loans and the more money you can be allowed to borrow.

Properly used, credit can be a beautiful thing. An excellent credit score can open doors to home ownership, business loans, car owner-ship, and other ways to leverage huge amounts of cash you may never be able to earn otherwise at low interest rates. In this way, you can build wealth. You can obtain wealth through loans to invest in prop-erty, business, and education, allowing you to make more money than you ever could have using your own savings and your 9-5 job alone.

This is among the secrets that the wealthy know. It often isn't neces-sary to save huge quantities of money in order to acquire wealth. Instead, if you have a truly solid business plan, it is often possible to *borrow* large sums of money, and turn that money into a much larger sum than you originally borrowed through your sound investment.

But that's only possible if you have a good credit score, and the access to good lines of credit that brings. If you *don't* have that, you can instead find yourself actively punished in areas ranging from housing to employment for failing to demonstrate that you can borrow money and then pay it back.

In my early 20s, it seemed like I was doomed. I had all kinds of debts, bills, and felt like I'd never get ahead. And with employers checking my credit report before deciding whether to hire me, it seemed as though I wouldn't be able to get a good paying job to pay off my debts until after I'd paid off my debts. It was a Catch-22. And I had a child to support: failure was not an option.

I began to research the problem. How exactly had my credit score gotten so bad? That was simple: by charging money on credit cards and not paying it back, not paying my bills on time or at all, and carelessly dismissing my student loans.

But how did I fix it? That was more complicated. It involved not only paying my debts, but also navigating a complicated maze of letter-writing, credit monitoring, interest rate calculations, and numerous other complex and time-consuming tasks.

But there was a silver lining: the fact that these tasks existed meant that there was something I could do. I didn't have to just wait for money to magically appear and hope my credit score got better. So I threw myself into doing the things I learned about through my research. I threw myself into it with a passion.

Slowly but surely, I began to see progress. I learned from many iterations of trial and error, where I tried something that just plain didn't work or even made the situation *worse*. I'll share my mistakes with you in this book, so you won't have to make them all yourself.

By 2014, I was able to finance a newer Nissan Maxima. In 2016, my heart sang as I closed on ownership of my first home—a four-bedroom house with a low-interest fixed-rate mortgage and only paid $422 out of my pocket on the closing date!

My home ownership was possible because of the way I had built up my credit score, and learned to use credit to grow my wealth instead of growing debts, over the preceding years. I'd gone from being a broke single mom struggling through college to a four-bedroom homeowner with big plans to continue growing generational wealth for my family. I had essentially jumped straight from one socioeconomic class to another.

And without my credit education, this would never have been possible.

In this book, I want to teach you everything I learned during those years of struggle. I will even supply you with letter templates, phone scripts, and a list of vetted and reliable tools to use to repair, protect, and build your credit so that you can do the same to establish your own wealth.

We will close this book with a brief discussion of business credit—a tool that is different from personal credit, but which can be used for the same astonishing wealth-building purposes, and which most people never learn anything about.

All I ask is that you read through this book carefully, and apply any of its techniques which might improve your fortunes. I want you to succeed and build wealth as I have done. If the necessary steps prove too time-consuming or difficult for where you are right now, my business can help you with the labor.

Together, we can change your destiny.

CHAPTER 2
HOW CAN I BENEFIT FROM CREDIT?

YOUR CREDIT SCORE is very much like your track record in a competitive sport. An expert on the game can glance at somebody's credit history and know exactly how good they are at playing the credit game. A credit expert can estimate that person's chances of winning in specific circumstances because they can see what challengers they've already faced and how they fared.

This is important, because the better a bank or creditor thinks you are at the game, the more money they will give you. Now it's not a free gift—you have to pay it back. But how *much* you have to pay back, and how much you're given in the first place, will largely depend on your credit score.

Say, for example, you want to buy a house. To do this, on paper, you need $300,000, because that's how much the house costs. Obviously not a lot of people have $300,000 lying around. But someone with an excellent credit score could get a $300,000 mortgage, which will allow them to live in the house and claim ownership while they gradually pay the house off over time. The same holds true for business loans, cars, and countless other forms of credit.

In fact, it's a little-known truth that the very wealthy rarely spend their own money to make money—they typically use their excellent credit scores to take out mortgages and loans, which they can use their business knowledge to turn into much, much more money than they borrowed in the first place. This is how they become wealthy.

And this is what my series of books are designed to teach you to do.

Now don't jump the gun and immediately go out and procure a massive loan which you try to turn a profit on. The only reason the very wealthy are able to succeed in this is that:

1. They have excellent credit, and;
2. They have insider knowledge of how to identify and use profitable investments. You *can* gain this knowledge, but it will take an excellent credit score and probably also a few years unless you have a mentor to fast-track the process. Think of this as a long game. If you are ambitious about making massive wins, you have to make your early moves carefully and strategically.

Why is having excellent credit so important before you try to grow your wealth with mortgages or business loans? Well, your credit score will impact your interest payment.

When asked what the most powerful force in the universe was, Albert Einstein is widely reported to have said "compound interest." That probably wasn't the answer the interviewer was expecting from a physicist, but it goes to show how powerful interest rates can be. "Compound interest" refers to the amount of money you pay—or *get* paid—over time as a consequence of someone borrowing money.

The trick about interest rates is that they often look tiny. The difference between a good interest rate and a bad interest rate may be just a few percent of the total amount you are borrowing. You may look at that few percent and think, "I can afford to pay that."

But the trick is, the way that interest adds up over time when it is applied monthly or yearly to your loan or mortgage comes out to be much more than a few percent. On that $300,000 house I mentioned earlier, having a high interest rate might mean you end up paying a full $99,000 more for the same property than you would have paid if you'd had a lower interest rate!

This is how the rich get richer and those of us who aren't rich, all too often, get poorer.

But the good news is, you don't need to be rich to have an excellent credit score and get excellent interest rates. Anyone can do it. You just need to know how.

Just like any competitive sport, having a great credit track record is a learned skill. How good you get at the game is determined by the amount of time, effort, and strategy you put into winning.

In this chapter we'll investigate the underlying logic of credit scores —how banks and creditors decide how much money to lend you, how they decide what interest rates to charge, and why they think any of that is a good idea. This underlying logic will help us understand the specific steps we need to take to get into the same credit tier as the ultra-wealthy.

WHY LEND MONEY AT ALL?

At this point you might be asking yourself, "Why would banks and creditors lend money at all? What's in it for them?" After all, we're rarely thrilled when a friend or family member comes and asks us to lend them cash.

The answer to that question is the most powerful force in the universe: interest.

Suppose you're a bank or creditor. You lend a lot of money to a lot of different people. And all of those people end up paying you back *more* than you leant them, because you charge interest. What looks like just a few percent interest on that $300,000 mortgage means you get paid $99,000 more than you leant out over time. And you may be making such loans to hundreds of thousands or even millions of people if you're a big lender.

Essentially, the more money you lend, the more money you make, usually. This is why banks are such powerful financial players.

But this puts you in something of a competition with borrowers.

Borrowers want you to lend them money so they can live in that $300,000 house, and someday maybe sell it to get $300,000 or more in cash without having to put up $300,000 cash up front. But they *don't* want to be charged $99,000 in interest. They want to get the lowest interest rate possible.

They do this by having an excellent credit score. Here's why and how that works.

Remember when I noted above that the more money you lend, the more money you make as a bank or creditor? But I appended a "usually." That "usually" comes from the fact that a certain percentage of borrowers won't pay back the money they borrow. This represents a loss for the bank or creditor. Obviously, banks wish to avoid such losses.

They do this by measuring how good a person is at paying back money they borrow. If someone frequently fails to pay their bills, the banks must try to cover their potential losses from that person by charging them a sky-high credit rate. This can even be profitable if the bank actually gets many people to pay these sky-high credit rates over time.

If someone always pays their bills promptly, on the other hand, the equation changes. This is someone who a bank or creditor can be pretty sure will pay back what they're leant. This means this person can be offered a much lower interest rate without risk to the bank. And, more importantly, it means the bank *has* to offer them a lower interest rate.

Why? Because everybody wants to lend money to these repayment superstars. Their excellent credit means they are virtually guaranteed to pay back what they borrow, with interest. That means that every bank and credit card out there is competing to lend these people money and get it paid back with just a little bit of interest. Whoever offers the lowest interest rate may just be the one to capture that person's business.

By paying bills promptly on time and knowing other techniques to ensure your credit score is as high as possible, you become one of the borrowers that banks and creditors compete with each other to lend to.

You have such a good track record at the credit game that different "teams"—banks or creditors—will make you competing offers to try to get you to play for them.

If you have a poor credit score, on the other hand, you might suffer the classic tragedy of that unathletic kid on the playground: you might get picked for the team last, and given all the worst positions to play.

The unfortunate side effect of this system is that it often favors the wealthy—those who already have so much money that paying the bills is not a challenge for them—while harming those living in poverty, forcing them to pay much more for pretty much everything they might desire to possess via high interest rates.

The good news is, we can fix your interest rate and make you a credit superstar no matter how little money you have. In this game, strategy is even more important than raw power. Let's start learning how to do that now.

HOW TO BUILD YOUR CREDIT SCORECARD

If you were a coach deciding what players to hire for your team, what factors might you look at? You might look at things like:

- How many games they had won in the past.
- How many teams they had played for successfully.
- How frequently they screwed up, costing the team points.

This is quite similar to how banks and creditors evaluate you as a borrower. The exact formula used to determine a FICO credit score—the most common credit score used by banks and creditors to determine whether to lend you money, and at what interest rate—goes something like this:

1. Payment history. This is basically your track record for winning games. A bill paid on time is a credit game won. A bill paid over 30 days late or not at all is a game lost. The more games you've won in the past, the more a bank or creditor wants you to play for their team. And the more they are willing to "pay" in terms of low interest rates

and other financial rewards to get you on their team. Payment history accounts for about 35% of your credit score.

One important thing to note here is that you can't win any games if you don't play. Some people assume they must have perfect credit because they have never borrowed money. If you never spend more money than you need, that's a really good sign for your financial responsibility, right?

But in the eyes of banks and creditors, the opposite is true. If no one has ever seen you pick up a ball, they're not just going to assume that you can make breathtaking plays. So you've got to borrow money and pay it back—you've got to play the game—in order to build credit. The key is to borrow money, not because you *need* to, but because you are doing it strategically to optimize your credit score.

We'll discuss the details of how to do this later.

2. Amounts owed. If someone owes a lot of money, that's not a great sign for you as a lender. *Why* do they owe so much money? Why haven't they paid more of it back yet? If I lend them money, are they going to be able to pay me back *and* pay back all these other people?

Think of this like a sports team hiring someone who they know already has a full-time commitment to another team. How much time and energy is that player really going to be able to give your team? You want someone who isn't overcommitted, and who you know has a lot of free time and energy to give your team a stellar performance.

As a borrower, you want to keep your credit utilization rate below 30%. That means that of the total amount of money you are allowed to charge on your credit card, for example, you're only using 30% or less. In general, lower is better. The more credit you have that you're not using, the more time and energy you have available to devote to any other team you apply for, so to speak. Having that availability makes you a better candidate.

This metaphor will break down a little bit in a minute, but for now that's a useful way to think of it.

Amounts owed—the less, the better—makes up about 30% of your credit score.

3. Credit history length. The more games you've played and won,

the better you look to a sports team. The longer you've been borrowing money and paying it back successfully, the better you look to a bank or creditor.

This is why it's so important to start building credit history with a credit card or loan *as soon as possible*. The longer you make payments successfully, the better your credit score gets over time.

But don't go out and get any old loan or credit card right now! In the chapters to come, I will share some specific credit card and loan options that offer great benefits to people with low credit scores which will allow you to start building positive lines of credit and gain maximum benefits.

Learning which loans and cards will help vs. hurt your credit and finances is an integral part of the game strategy. Read just a few more chapters to learn to improve your credit score without paying interest rates to profit somebody else.

4. Credit mix. This is where the sports metaphor breaks down a little. When hiring an athlete, you usually want that athlete to be playing *only* for your team. But banks and creditors want you to have *multiple* creditors, if only so that you can prove that you're already paying multiple accounts successfully.

Think of it like if sports had an option to keep a player on retainer. This player is not being called upon often enough to negatively impact their ability to perform for you, but the fact that so many teams want him—and the fact that they perform well for all of them—makes you really, really want him on your team.

Banks and creditors like to see that you regularly pay a variety of different types of bills. They like you to have a loan or two under your belt, as well as multiple credit cards.

This is a dangerous mix for someone who isn't very good at budgeting; they could easily use all these sources of borrowed money to get deeply in debt with no way out. But that's precisely what proves your skill to creditors; if you can juggle that many accounts and win every time, you must be really really excellent.

Think of a player who wins games for five different teams, reliably, every single month. If that person went looking for another team to join wouldn't you really want them? Wouldn't you offer them a super-great paycheck—or interest rate and rewards package—to join you?

Credit mix makes up about 10% of your credit score.

5. New credit. Let's extend the sports metaphor here: if a player *just* started playing for a bunch of new teams in a short span of time, you'd be kind of nervous about them, wouldn't you? What if they've over-committed? What if they can't perform well for all of you at the same time, and they just haven't figured that out yet?

Opening a lot of new lines of credit, or attempting to do so, is a red flag for lenders. It suggests that you might be having a lot of trouble paying bills, or might be trying to borrow more money than you can feasibly pay back.

This can be especially frustrating, because shopping around for just a single loan can *look* like you're applying for too many lines of credit —or *not*, depending on how strategically you act. This once happened to me: I only needed one loan, but because of the way I went about applying for one, it looked to my creditors like I was seeking *dozens* of loans. My credit score took a big hit because of that.

We will explore how to be strategic in applying for new lines of credit, to ensure you get the loan you need without sending out multiple applications that raise red flags for lenders, later in this book.

Your number of recent credit applications make up about 10% of your FICO score.

Having read this description, perhaps you now have a better idea of just how important strategy is to the credit game. Having wealth already in your pocket is the easiest way to make sure you pay your bills on time, but decisions about which bills to pay first, how to strate-gically use your existing lines of credit, when to borrow money and from whom, and how to apply for loans you need can all make your credit score better—or worse.

In this way, someone with lots of money but little knowledge of the game can end up with less borrowing power and higher interest rates than someone with little disposable income but excellent strategic knowledge. If you play strategically, you can end up with the kinds of mortgages and business loans that build a legacy of generational wealth for your family, even if you have little to no cash.

Now that we understand how banks and creditors evaluate us as players, let's learn exactly how to play the game.

CHAPTER 3
WINNING AT PAYMENT HISTORY

THE VERY FIRST thing many people need to tackle is improving their payment history. Poor payment history happens when you have credit cards, loans, or other bills that you have paid late or not at all. Any type of creditor including doctors and hospitals, universities and student loan companies, and many others can report you to credit bureaus in a way that harms your credit score if you don't pay them.

Any of them *can*. But not all of them *do*. That's one aspect of credit strategy.

Obviously, if you had a ton of money you wouldn't be having problems with payment history in the first place. This can make tackling this problem particularly daunting, because it's not like you're not paying simply because you don't feel like it. If you could magically produce enough money to pay all of these bills, you would have done it already.

So what we're going to talk about here is how to strategize to pay the bills which are hurting you most *first*. Eventually, we will want to pay all of them; but the more high-impact bills we take care of, the easier it will become to take care of the rest. We'll consider factors like:

- Interest rates. Are you paying way more money in interest on some bills than others? If so, we'll take care of those bills first so that you're charged less money in interest. That will free up more money to pay other bills.
- Late fees. Are you accruing late fees or other penalties on certain types of bills? These will eat into your overall budget and make it harder to pay off anything at all. So we'll also take care of those first.
- Credit score impact. Are some of your creditors harming your credit score more than others? If so, we will prioritize those. You may even be able to open low interest rate lines of credit that you can use to help pay off or consolidate your other bills. This can help get your credit score up by removing negative items from your report.
- Seven-year statutory limit. Did you know that most derogatory marks on your credit report should be removed after a period of seven years? This may be very important for you if you have outstanding debts which are five or more years old. You may not need to pay these in order for them to disappear.

Attacking your payment history strategically will allow you to save a lot of money compared to simply randomly paying whatever creditor is being most insistent at a given time. That in turn will make it easier for you to get a stellar payment history quickly. So let's get started.

THE STATUTORY LIMIT

One of the most important things to know in the credit game is that all negative reporting has a statutory limit. This means that a negative item cannot remain on your credit report for more than a certain period of time.

Most of the time, this makes little difference: if you have negative items on your credit report and you wish to buy a house, rent an apartment, apply for a business loan, buy or lease a car, or get a job which requires a credit check *before* the seven-year statutory limit occurs, you will want to resolve these negative items and/or pursue options to raise your credit score immediately such as those we discuss here. But there are also times when you can use the statutory limit to your advantage.

If a negative item on your credit report is already six years old and you owe a lot of money on that bill, it might make sense to simply wait for it to fall off your report before making a major financial move or trying to contact that company. If *not* paying this bill means saving tens of thousands of dollars, waiting a few months for that derogatory mark to disappear may make more sense than paying.

One other piece of information that is vital to know is this: if you contact your creditor about your debt, you restart the age of the account. This means that the clock starts counting down from "zero" again, and it will take seven years *after the last date of activity.*

This is why it's important to pay attention to the age of your accounts before taking action on them. If an account of yours is already five or six years old, contacting the creditor to pay or negotiate may result in losing your ability to have the red mark automatically removed from your report in just one or two years without the necessity to pay.

Keep this in mind when filling out the following chapters, which will invite you to make a strategy to pay off your outstanding debts while saving as much money as possible. If a debt is already six years old and you don't need your credit history improved immediately in the next few months, you can omit that debt from your calculations as it should soon automatically disappear from your credit report on its own.

KNOW YOUR INTEREST RATES

If you have taken out multiple loans, there's a good chance they have different interest rates. Do you know what your interest rate is on each loan, mortgage, and credit card you have? If not, I want you to go through your files and look up that information right now. Here's a little worksheet you can fill out so we can keep track:

Credit Line 1: _____

    Interest rate: _____% **Amount owed:** _____

    Credit Line 2: _____

    Interest rate: _____% **Amount owed:** _____

    Credit Line 3: _____

    Interest rate: _____% **Amount owed:** _____

    Credit Line 4: _____

    Interest rate: _____% **Amount owed:** _____

    Credit Line 5: _____

    Interest rate: _____% **Amount owed:** _____

    Credit Line 6: _____

    Interest rate: _____% **Amount owed:** _____

Now, here's a bit of simple math: the higher the interest rate on any given credit line, the more money that loan is costing you for every single month there remains a balance. This is very significant, especially since paying that interest over time might be stopping you from paying *other* bills, which might in turn be causing you more interest and late fees.

This is what I refer to as "the interest snowball." When you are paying more than necessary in interest, this cost can end up multiplying and costing you way more than you realize in interest payments and late fees over time.

In order to get your interest payments down, we're going to prioritize paying off your highest-interest lines of credit *first*. The moment those lines of credit are fully paid, poof—your interest payments disappear!

Now, you don't want to stop paying other bills entirely in order to pay off a high-interest line of credit. But you might consider going down to the minimum payment you can make without being punished with late fees or interest rate hikes on other lines of credit in order to put as much money as possible toward making the highest-interest debt disappear.

You might also consider temporarily cutting down on unnecessary expenses in order to achieve this. There may be pleasures you would not want to go without permanently, but if skipping them for a few weeks allows you to eliminate a high-interest loan, you can think of the temporary deprivation as an investment in having a lot more spending money in the future.

Let's take a moment to rank your open credit lines by interest rate, in order from highest to lowest. Place the loan with the highest interest rate at the top of the list, and the loan with the lowest interest rate at the bottom:

Credit Line 1: _____ **Interest Rate:** _____%

Credit Line 2: _____ **Interest Rate:** _____%

Credit Line 3: _____ **Interest Rate:** _____%

Credit Line 4: _____ **Interest Rate:** _____%

Credit Line 5: _____ **Interest Rate:** _____%

Credit Line 6: _____ **Interest Rate:** _____%

Now, focus on getting each of these lines of credit completely paid off as quickly as possible, moving from top to bottom. This will save you the most money in the long run, and saving money means having money available to make credit power moves.

While you're eliminating high-interest lines of credit that you already owe, it's also a good idea to start comparatively shopping in the event that you need to open a new line of credit for some reason.

It's a good idea to avoid taking out a new loan or line of credit at this time, because if you wait a few weeks or months until we have implemented the other steps in this workbook you will get much better offers. But if you simply must take out a new loan or line of credit, follow this protocol to get the best results:

1. Research until you find at least *six* different options that are available to you to procure this financing.
2. Of the six options you find, carefully review their terms and interest rates.
3. Choose the option with the *lowest* interest rate to add to your credit roster.

Again, I would advise waiting until you have worked all the way through this book to ensure that you get the best possible terms and make the most strategic plays. But if life happens in the meantime, be conscious of the terms you are agreeing to and the fact that there are always multiple financing options available to you.

KNOW YOUR LATE FEES & OVERDRAFT FEES

Late fees are another way we can lose more money than we realize. These often come out to cost us less than interest rates because they are typically small, flat, fixed fees. But paying several late fees can add up to over $100 per month *just* going to late fees, and not helping you afford anything you want!

Late fees can also apply to things that interest rates typically don't, such as late fees on rent payments. Some creditors may charge *both* interest rates and late fee payments, which can add up very quickly.

For each line of credit or monthly bill that you are struggling to pay, look up what your fee for late payment is and list them here. This will help tell you what bills you should prioritize paying first if you can't pay all of them on time in order to save the most money:

Bill 1: _____

Late fee amount: _____$ Kicks in after what date? ___/___/_____

Bill 2: _____

Late fee amount: _____$ Kicks in after what date? ___/___/_____

Bill 3: _____

Late   fee   amount: _____$ Kicks   in   after   what   date?
___/___/_____

Bill 4: _____

Late   fee   amount: _____$ Kicks   in   after   what   date?
___/___/_____

Bill 5: _____

Late   fee   amount: _____$ Kicks   in   after   what   date?
___/___/_____

Bill 6: _____

Late   fee   amount: _____$ Kicks   in   after   what   date?
___/___/_____

Keep these amounts and dates in mind, and try to strategically balance your budget to avoid having to pay any late fees. If this requires short term sacrifices, remember that your finances will grow more and more powerful as you eliminate late fees and interest payments from the amount you are paying each month moving into the future.

There is one final, very important consideration to take into account when prioritizing which bills to pay first. This is a factor that can work powerfully for you or against you if you use it properly.

KNOW WHO IS REPORTING TO THE CREDIT BUREAUS

What if I told you that not every single party you owe money to may report you to a credit bureau? It's not a good idea to plan to skip out on bills, but if you are overwhelmed with debt and need to pay down your most pressing debts fast, knowing which, if any of your creditors will not negatively impact your credit score can be very powerful.

The best way to know which bills are or are not harming your credit score is to check your credit report. Your credit report will show exactly which creditors have reported you as late-paying or non-paying, harming your credit track record. Some creditors will report you quickly and aggressively, even if you only owe them a tiny amount; others, for various reasons, may elect not to do so even if you owe them thousands of dollars.

If a negative remark appears on your credit report, sometimes you can quickly raise your credit score by paying that bill. But first, you will need to call the creditor and specifically request that they report a change in your payment status to the credit bureau. Be sure to get this agreement in writing! Once they agree, if you get the payment status reported properly, it is as though your late payment or nonpayment never happened.

If you can catch a late bill while it's still in collections before it hits your credit file, that's even better. In that case, you can sometimes negotiate payment for pennies on the dollar!

Now, you've solved the nonpayment problem, so that loss is removed from your scorecard and replaced by a win. We will cover exactly how to make this happen later in this book.

Since the only way to be certain which bills are harming your credit score is to look at your credit report, let's investigate how to do that next.

CHAPTER 4
CHECKING YOUR CREDIT REPORT

THERE ARE many services out there which claim to offer free access to your credit score and credit report. While some of these can be helpful, unfortunately, not all of them are reliable enough to be your primary source of information.

As with any bureaucratic system, mistakes can creep into the process of calculating a credit report. For this reason, third party reports offered by sites like Credit Karma and Credit Sesame may not actually match what potential landlords, employers, and lenders will see when they file a formal credit check to make a decision about whether to allow you to rent a property, take out a mortgage or business loan, or any number of countless essential operations that can be affected by your credit score.

Here are some of my favorite sources for accurate information about your credit score, and what nonpayment items might be negatively affecting it. Once you have this information, you can target these negative items for repair.

ANNUALCREDITREPORT.COM

AnnualCreditReport.com is the official website to check your credit report. This website is actually regulated by the government, which requires that it provide a free credit report to everyone at least once per year. During emergency times like the COVID-19 pandemic, the government may even mandate that free scores be made available to people more frequently to allow them to stay on top of their credit during times of economic upheaval.

That's how important credit reports are: free access to them is considered a fundamental right that is protected by the government. And the government *must* mandate that they be made freely available at least once per year, because they are valuable enough that many people would pay for access.

As of this writing, all three credit bureaus are offering free credit reports on a weekly basis instead of an annual one due to the economic hardship posed by COVID-19. Since we cannot guarantee that will last forever, I will write the rest of this chapter with the assumption that the credit bureaus will eventually revert to offering these scores only once per year.

One important thing to know is that you *don't* have to pay for access to your credit report once per year. Some credit bureau websites may display misleading messages implying that you can't see your credit score or report at all unless you subscribe to a paid service. This is not the case: if you go to a website and receive such a message, hunt around until you find a link that allows you to go to your free credit report instead. This must be offered to you freely. It is a federal requirement.

The fact that, in typical times, the government only requires that you be offered your credit report freely once per year can be an impediment to some people. How are we to know if our credit building efforts are working if we can only access our reliable report once per year?

Well, there's good news: there are three different bureaus which provide FICO credit score estimates to banks, landlords, employers, etc. And you get to access *each one* for free once per year. That means that, if you only check one at a time, you can check one report every four months for free.

The three major bureaus which provide credit estimates to potential lenders are Equifax, Experian, and Transunion. Each of these organizations use proprietary formulas to try to calculate your FICO score based on the credit score factors we've discussed so far. Their reports may slightly differ from each other because of the different algorithms and/or accounts reporting, but the scores usually come out to be within a few points of each other across all three bureaus.

Now, just knowing your credit score does not do much if you don't know what specific unpaid bills may be harming it. Your credit report, when you access it through AnnualCreditReport.com, will list in detail *all* negative marks against your credit history.

It will list information about what creditor reported each negative mark, and that is the information you need: once you know who has reported you to a credit bureau for nonpayment, you know who you have to talk to and pay off or challenge ASAP to get the loss on your scorecard turned into a win.

To get started, why don't you get online and access your credit report right now? Access it for *only* one of the three bureaus, so that you will be able to access the other two later in the year.

When you open your credit report, you may see a list of complex acronyms indicating different types of problems that a credit report can have. Don't panic: that's not a list of all the problems with *your* report. It's a key so you can understand any problems that may appear on your report. Scroll down to see your personal credit history.

If you access your credit report through one of the three bureau websites, you can access a screen which will show your current credit score with that bureau, as well as a list of any late payments, debt collections, or other problems that have been reported to the credit bureau. This is the list you can use to address each of these negative marks and change your credit status to "paid as agreed." We will address some specific steps you can take to do this in a later chapter.

You may also see things on your credit report that don't make sense. Perhaps there are some accounts reported that definitely don't belong to you. This can happen for two reasons:

- There was a paperwork error involving someone with a similar name. People who share a first and last name with a close relative are especially prone to such errors.
- Your identity was stolen. In this case, someone managed to access enough of your personal, confidential information to open accounts while pretending to be you.

In both cases, there are solutions you can apply to get these incorrect items removed from your credit report. We'll discuss how to do this in a later chapter, too.

Are you comfortable with your credit report? If so, make a list of any problems reported in your report such as late payments or non-payments. Like the lists we made in the previous chapter, this will function as a master list to help you decide who to pay or challenge first. The faster you address these debts, the sooner you can turn these losses into wins on your scorecard.

Since larger debts don't necessarily harm your credit score more, you may wish to start by paying off small debts that appear on your credit report immediately and work your way up. Getting a $30 late utility bill paid off and removed from your credit report can be a very liberating feeling!

Problem 1: _____

Problem 2: _____

Problem 3: _____

Problem 4: _____

Problem 5: _____

Problem 6: _____

Now that we have opened the box that is your credit report, we will briefly discuss the other factors in addition to payment history that affect your credit report. Then we will investigate specific tools to get your payment status changed to "paid as agreed" and to dispute incorrect red marks on your credit score.

CHAPTER 5
WINNING CREDIT HISTORY LENGTH

WHEN YOU'RE CONSIDERING HIRING a new player for your team, you want as much evidence as possible that they can help your team. If the player has played many games in the past, that gives you a lot of opportunity to see how they perform.

In the game of credit, we can think of the number of months of credit history under your belt as the number of games you have played. That means that someone with five or ten years of experience paying off credit lines under their belt is more likely to be picked for the good "teams"—or in this case, the good mortgages, credit cards, and car loans—than someone with few or no months of credit history under their belt.

If you haven't played many games of repayment before, how can banks have confidence that you have what it takes to pay off a $300,000 house? The answer is, they can't. And they probably won't lend you enough money to buy such a house.

This means that to create the best possible opportunities for yourself, you want to start building your credit history right now. This means finding a loan, a credit card, or both that you can pay off regularly each month to get some wins on your record.

Now, you don't want just *any* loan or credit card. As we discussed in the last chapter, some credit cards and loans offer excellent terms such that you lose nothing by using them. Others are downright predatory, with interest rates and enforcement terms that can easily harm your credit in the long run.

So how do you find a really good "team" to play for if you don't already have a lot of credit history to prove you're a good player? The good news is, there are loans and credit cards created specifically to help new players like yourself. Here are some of the best options.

To build credit history fast, you'll want to start playing for 3-5 different "teams" ASAP. This allows you to "win" 3-5 games each month, which shows banks and credit card companies that you're good at repaying the money you borrow on time.

We'll spend the rest of this chapter talking about my three favorite "teams" for new players to start with. If you do all three, you'll start building credit fast while paying little to no interest and with no risk of losing your assets.

RENTREPORTERS.COM

There's a good chance you're already paying rent to a landlord. It may surprise you to learn that these payments are *not* reported to credit bureaus. This can be a good thing or a bad thing, depending on your situation: if you struggle to pay rent on time, that won't harm your credit score. But it also means that all your on-time payments don't *help* your credit score. Unless you use RentReporters.com

This website allows you to sign up to have your monthly on-time rent payments reported as "wins" to the credit bureaus. If you are making rent payments on time and think you will be able to keep doing so for at least the next year, this is an excellent tool because it builds credit history without adding any new bills at all to your life. You simply get credit for the bills you're already paying.

If you don't pay rent because you own your home and you have a mortgage, good news: your mortgage payments are *already* being reported as "wins" to credit bureaus because they technically count as repayments on the money you agreed to pay the bank when you bought the property.

If you have been struggling to pay rent on time, or think you might struggle to do so in the next year, that is the only reason to *avoid* signing up for this service. We want to report wins on your record, so if you aren't certain of winning at paying rent, keep that particular game off your scorecard.

Whether you sign up for RentReporter.com or not, these following options can help you build your credit without the cost and risk associated with typical credit cards or loans.

CREDITBUILDERCARD.COM

CreditBuilderCard.com offers what is called a secured line of credit. A "secured" line means that you can get it even if you have a very poor credit score, because you promise to use the value of something you already own to pay the credit card company if you can't pay them back on time through normal means.

Most secured lines of credit can be very risky. Some secured credit lines may ask you to use things like your house or your retirement fund as "security," basically obligating you to give them these assets if you can't pay your bill. This is obviously very risky if you're agreeing to a huge amount of security in exchange for a line of credit.

However, CreditBuilderCard.com is built specifically to offer credit lines to people with poor credit scores without a big risk. For the Credit Builder card, the "security" you promise is just a one-time $200 deposit that you pay, which Credit Builder will use to cover any losses they may incur if you spend money on your credit card and can't pay it back.

The great thing about this is that they don't do a "hard inquiry"—a type of background check used by most lenders and credit card companies. This is important because hard inquiries actually hurt your credit score. This is because credit bureaus may assume that applying for credit cards or loans means you are struggling to pay your bills as-is, so they deduct a few points from your score each time you do so.

CreditBuilderCard.com does *not* run this kind of background check, so you will not lose those points by applying to open an account with them. In fact, none of the resources listed in this chapter run such inquiries, which means you can open three lines of credit to start "winning" three games every single month fast without losing any points to inquiries, the way you would if you applied for a normal commercial credit card or loan.

Now, CreditBuilderCard.com *does* report to major credit bureaus like any other credit card. That means that, just like RentReporter.com, your credit score may actually be harmed if you make purchases with your Credit Builder card and then don't pay your bill for this credit card on time.

The good news is, you choose how much you spend on this card and how much you subsequently have to pay back. I recommend simply charging a small expense like a meal or a cup of coffee on your Credit Builder card once a month or once every couple of months. This ensures that you will be able to win your credit game every single month by successfully making a payment for the full amount you owe.

One useful thing to know is that, when it comes to credit cards, credit bureaus don't care if you are paying back $25 or $500—both count as an equal repayment win, assuming that you have met the minimum payment requirement and stayed below 10% of your total credit card limit and you actually do pay the full amount off on time.

Because large and small payments both count as equal victories in the eyes of credit bureaus, it pays to use your credit card for just a tiny monthly purchase until you have built up the kind of credit score that allows you to have a high credit limit and an excellent interest rate if you don't pay off your full balance each month.

This next option is similar to CreditCardBuilder.com in its benefits for your credit score. It comes with the added cost of a fixed monthly payment, but also the added benefit that you get all the money you pay this lender back at the end of your "loan"!

SELFLENDER.COM

SelfLender.com is an ingenious idea built specifically to help people build credit without losing money. SelfLender.com combines the credit history benefits of taking out a loan with the money-saving benefits of a savings account.

First, you apply for a loan through the SelfLender.com website. Next, you choose how much to "borrow" and how long you want to take to "repay" the amount. I'm putting "borrow" and "repay" in quotation marks because you won't actually be borrowing or repaying anything; instead, you will be making payments into what is essentially a savings account.

Your payments to this savings account will be reported to credit bureaus as though you were paying off a loan. As long as you meet your savings goals and make the payments required by the contract you chose, you will be marked down as having a loan repayment win for the month.

But instead of getting money up-front which you then have to pay back, SelfLender.com essentially does things in reverse. You get the money you've paid into your savings account at the *end* of the process, and you don't have to pay it back since it is your money that you've saved up.

Pretty good deal, right? You get to build credit history with no hard inquiry, and at the end of the process you get paid a bunch of money that you have saved up for yourself through your monthly payments.

One of the best parts of the design is that, since you have not actually borrowed money that you are now obligated to pay back, you can cancel your account and stop paying off your "loan" at any time if you need to. This means that if something happens and you can't save up the full amount you planned, your credit score won't show this as a failure. Instead of taking losses on your scorecard for each month you can't pay, you'll simply show as taking a break from the game for personal reasons.

This tool builds your credit *and* your savings with none of the usual costs or risks associated with taking out a loan. There's no reason not to do it, and every reason to apply for an account today.

Remember, you'll be building skill at saving money in addition to building credit history. The money you save by paying yourself through SelfLender.com can even be used to pay off other lines of credit once you finish paying off your loan and the money you've paid in is returned to you.

KIKOFF.COM

KikOff.com is the last credit booster tool we'll be discussing in this chapter. Here you can sign up for an account and instantly get approved for a $500 line of credit. This is another provider that does not do a hard inquiry to check your scorecard, which means that applying with them will not cause your score to lose points. They do not require a minimum credit score and are an interest-free service with no additional fees.

KikOff.com also offers financial wellness ebooks and other self-help products with price tags starting between $10-$20. Their products require a minimum monthly payment of about only $2 per month which keeps their program affordable and easily manageable. They report each monthly payment to the three major credit bureaus. Each purchase helps build your credit month after month.

I often recommend that my clients set up a Visa gift card with at least $25 on it, then set their KikOff account to autopay from this gift card. This way you don't have to think about making your monthly payments—they are automatically withdrawn from your gift card—but you also don't get surprise charges on your primary bank account which may result in overdraft fees.

If you choose to use this approach, just ensure that you check back often enough to ensure that the Visa gift card remains loaded so you don't accidentally miss a payment!

NOW YOU'RE WINNING

If you use all three of these options, you will have three of the 3-5 lines of credit recommended by credit bureaus to build credit fast! And you will have done it all without losing any points to hard inquiries or taking on the risks of a high interest rate or a loan you can't pay back. Excellent work!

As your credit score rises as a result of meeting your commitments to pay rent, pay off that monthly cup of coffee you charge on your credit card, and pay yourself a few bucks each month in savings, you will find that you begin to qualify for better and better interest rates on loans and credit cards. This means you'll pay less money back for any money you borrow to buy a car or home or start a business.

You'll also qualify to borrow more and more money at a time as you demonstrate that you are capable of paying back what you borrow. This will allow you to have more robust emergency credit cards to fall back on in a time of crisis, or to qualify for loans on bigger and better homes and cars and more ambitious business ideas, especially when mixed with viable cash flow.

This is the secret that the wealthy know. They build credit cautiously and meticulously, then use it strategically to make the investments they know will pay off for their families for generations.

If you play your cards right, you can access huge amounts of wealth, which you can then invest strategically to gain more wealth, after a few years of meticulous credit building.

Just remember: this is a game of knowledge and skill. If you are not starting off with a huge amount of wealth to fall back on, it is especially important that you study all you can so that you can make the smartest choices and not fall for predatory lenders or scammers who might seek to profit at your expense with bad "investment" opportunities.

Study this game for a few years and you will become a wealth-building expert. I will be here to help you along the way.

CHAPTER 6
WINNING AT CREDIT MIX

BELIEVE IT OR NOT, if you've followed the steps in the previous chapter, you have already won at credit mix! But this is an important part of your credit score, so it's important that you now understand exactly *how* you did that.

"Credit mix" refers to having different types of credit lines that you are successfully paying off each month. Think of it as demonstrating a variety of different skills in the game of credit. If you are a coach recruiting for a team, you want a player who has shown that they can successfully execute many skills and techniques. A player who is very, very good at a wide range of skills will likely be offered a better contract than someone who is very good at just one skill. The same is true when it comes to loans and credit cards.

How do you demonstrate a variety of skills in the game of credit? Well, you do it by paying off credit lines with different sorts of payment terms. Here are some different types of credit accounts you can get to demonstrate that you have a diverse skill set. You may recognize these terms from the previous chapter:

INSTALLMENT LOANS

Installment loans are loans where you pay a fixed amount to a creditor each month. This demonstrates to banks and credit card companies that you are capable of paying significant amounts of money back over a long period of time. It shows that you are able to plan ahead and borrow only what you can pay back, even many months or years in advance.

A history of successfully paying off installment loans shows creditors that it is safe to lend you large amounts of money, because you won't let them down when it comes to repayment.

You may recognize this model from SelfLender.com in the previous chapter. You agreeing to pay a fixed amount to your savings account each month—and then actually doing it—will show credit bureaus that have this skill. Paying off a student loan or other type of loan with installment payments would show them the same thing, but with Self-Lender.com you don't pay interest on the money you "borrowed" and you are not in danger of showing losses on your scorecard if you can't pay.

Still, you are building and demonstrating the same kind of skill set necessary to pay off a student loan, home, car, or business loan. This means that lenders will be more likely to approve you for such loans in the future. The more you can demonstrate this skill through a long credit history or paying off more than one loan each month successfully, the more likely they are to offer you excellent interest rates and loan large amounts.

REVOLVING DEBT

Revolving debt refers to debts that change each month or are flexible. A common example of a revolving debt is a credit card, where you have the freedom to borrow and pay back as little as $0 or as much as thousands of dollars each month.

If loans show lenders that you have the skills of planning ahead and following through on long-term commitments, revolving debt shows lenders that you can be trusted with flexibility and freedom in your borrowing power. It shows that you will not borrow more than you can afford if given a high credit limit, and that if for some reason you *have* to charge a major purchase on a credit card you will reliably pay it back.

For you as a borrower, it's likely that you will benefit from having access to both long-term loans with fixed installment payments and flexible credit lines from which you can borrow a little or a lot each month depending on your needs. Flexible credit lines like credit cards usually don't have high enough limits to be used to buy a house or a new car, but they can be used to pay a few months' expenses in case of emergency or one-time business expenses.

Since you will benefit from access to the best terms and the highest limits on both installment and revolving types of credit accounts, it makes sense to demonstrate both types of skills to credit bureaus and future lenders.

You may recognize the credit card from Credit Builder in the previous chapter as a type of revolving account. This is one of several reasons I recommend that those who are able take advantage of all three resources in that chapter. By doing so, you will not only be winning three different credit games each month; you will be demonstrating both the skills needed to successfully obtain big home and business loans, and low-interest, high-limit credit cards from regular commercial lenders in the future.

OPEN ACCOUNTS

An open credit account is a credit account which allows for flexible spending like a credit card, but which requires the balance to be paid in full each month.

This type of credit line can be considered an expert-level display of skills: since you are not allowed to defer the balance you charge to future months under any circumstances, it really shows your ability to pay things back in a timely fashion.

I have not included suggestions for open account types here

because these are somewhat rare, and can be highly risky since it is easier for financial shortfalls to harm your credit score instead of helping it with this type of account. This type of account is not necessary to build credit rapidly, so I don't necessarily recommend it to my clients on the personal side. Instead, you may be better off simply opening another ordinary credit card once your credit score moves into the "good" range and you can qualify for low interest rates.

But because this is a type of account recognized by credit bureaus as a potential skill demonstrator, I wanted to let you know that these types of accounts exist and can speed up your credit building process if you don't have the kind of financial uncertainty that can lead to a missed payment.

MORTGAGE ACCOUNTS

Mortgage accounts, like open accounts, are an expert-level skill. They are considered separate from other types of loans because they may have special terms such as variable interest rates. The possibility that your interest rates may change in some mortgages, as well as the sheer size of the loan they represent, makes them another expert-level skill.

Like open accounts, I don't recommend that people take on a mortgage just to optimize their credit mix. Mortgages come with a lot of risk of harm to your credit score if you can't pay them, and as with open accounts, you are unlikely to qualify for favorable interest rates until *after* your credit is already good. As we discussed in a previous chapter, a poor interest rate on a mortgage can cost you over $100,000 in payments you could have avoided over time in some cases!

So if you don't already have a mortgage, don't go out and get one just to build your credit score faster. Wait until you have a good credit score that can get you a good interest rate and other favorable terms upfront. But if you do already have a mortgage, know that this is also counting positively toward your credit mix. You are showing real skill by paying that off!

GROWING YOUR CREDIT PORTFOLIO

Starting with RentReporter.com, a Credit Builder Card, a Self-Lender "loan," and Kikoff will put you on the road to growing credit fast by demonstrating multiple wins each month and a diverse mix of skills.

As your skills and your credit history grow, you will want to begin adding additional lines of credit for multiple reasons. These will help you build credit history faster; they will also give you more financial security and allow you to invest in yourself as you obtain low-interest credit cards and loans that can be used to cover emergency expenses, go to school, or start a business.

Just know that, as you do this, you will want to follow a few simple rules for best results:

1. Don't take out loans you don't need. You don't want to spend money you otherwise wouldn't *just* to boost your credit history. Instead, use SelfLender.com to demonstrate your loan skills, and only take out loans when there's something you actually want or need such as a car, degree, home, or business funding.

2. In loans and credit cards, play for the best possible interest rate. The higher your credit score is when you apply for a loan or credit card, the better interest rates and rewards you are likely to be offered. And different credit card companies and lenders will probably offer you different interest rates and repayment terms when the time comes to apply. As we've now seen, poor interest rates can cost you a lot of money with no benefit to yourself.

3. Research at least six competitors *before* you apply. As we mentioned in this chapter, hard inquiries that lenders perform when deciding whether they want to lend to you, and what terms they want to offer, actually harm your credit score. For that reason, compare what different credit card companies and lenders are offering to customers like yourself *before* you apply, so that you can be sure to apply to

only the one or two best options and minimize your hard inquiries. We'll discuss more about how to minimize hard inquiries when applying for loans in the next chapter

Congratulations! You're now all set to begin building your credit history with a robust credit mix, which means faster growth of your credit score. Now we'll discuss how to win in another column of the credit game score card: new credit.

CHAPTER 7
NEW CREDIT

WE MENTIONED EARLIER that coaches may be worried about hiring a player who seems overcommitted. If a player has just recently started playing for three new teams, how can you as a coach know that they will be able to keep up with all of those game schedules? You might also ask whether they're taking on so many contracts because they're struggling to pay their bills.

The same is true when it comes to opening new credit accounts. This is the reason why hard inquiries harm your credit score. Hard inquiries occur when a credit card company or potential lender reports to a credit bureau that you have asked for a new line of credit.

If you only do this once in a while, the benefits of having that new line of credit added to your credit history will probably outweigh the cost of the inquiry; but if you apply to many credit cards or lenders in a short span of time those hard inquiries can harm your credit score in a big way. And here's why.

Applying to many credit cards and lenders may be seen by credit bureaus that you're taking on more debt than you can manage. If you plan to start paying multiple loans and credit card bills at the same time—well, what are the chances that you will be successful in winning so many games for teams you're not used to playing for?

And there's another concern too. *Why* are you applying for all these loans and credit cards? Are you in big financial trouble, which might indicate that you might be less successful at paying all your bills in the future?

The frustrating part of this scoring system is that the number of hard inquiries reported to credit bureaus often doesn't accurately reflect how much money you actually want to borrow.

Having many hard inquiries doesn't necessarily mean that you want to take out six loans, or open six new credit cards; it could just mean that you *applied* to six lenders with a plan to only accept the best offer you got as part of a wise, strategic credit move.

But the credit bureaus don't know your intentions. If they get six hard inquiries, they'll assume you actually wanted all six credit cards. And there's nothing you can do about that, except study and strategize to get the absolute best offers with the absolute minimum number of hard inquiries.

As with all things in the credit game, knowledge is power. If you don't know how hard inquiries work, you can end up severely damaging your credit without even doing anything irresponsible. I have been in this exact position.

When I decided that my credit was good enough to get favorable terms on a car loan, I was so proud of myself. I had worked so hard to build my credit score, and it was about to pay off. I was going to be a responsible borrower: I was going to compare rates from a few different car dealerships to ensure I got the best possible terms and interest rates I could to save the most money.

There was just one problem: I didn't realize that every single dealership I applied with would send several hard inquiries to multiple lenders on my behalf. In effect, it would look to the credit bureaus like I was either unqualified to purchase a vehicle and desperate or trying to take out multiple different car loans at the same time.

Now, instead of just a few hard inquiries hitting my account, there were about 40 of them, all stemming from the three car dealers I had applied to!

My credit score was devastated, all because I decided to be a responsible comparative buyer when seeking a single modest car loan.

It wasn't fair. I didn't ask those dealers to behave that way on my behalf, and they weren't exactly looking out for my best interest by warning me that this would happen. They were only interested in getting the best possible loans *for themselves* on my behalf. I might have decided not to apply with them at all if I knew it would hurt my credit score. Too bad they weren't going to go out of their way to warn me about that either.

This was one of the hard lessons that compelled me to become a credit expert and educator. Studying what had happened in the aftermath, I learned that there was a way I could have gotten all the same comparative buying benefits while putting only *one* hard inquiry on my account. Here's how to do it!

SECURING FINANCING IN ADVANCE

What I didn't know when I applied for financing to all those car dealerships was that I *could* have come to them with financing already in hand. Then they would not have each sent out multiple inquiries on my behalf, and I would have gotten to compare their offers at no cost to myself.

How could I have done this? I could have gotten approved for a car loan through my bank or any other auto loan company or lender before I ever went to the dealerships.

If you have a bank account, you already have a relationship with a financial institution that may be willing to offer financing on items like car and business loans. Like all creditors, they will take your credit history into account: the better your score already is when you apply, the more favorable the terms you will get. But since they're the ones who get to hang onto your money in the bank, they may have more incentive to lend to you than a random lender would.

In fact, that in itself is a fact that few people know about banks. Banks are allowed to use the money you have sitting in your account to make investments of their own as long as they pay you back with interest. This, in fact, is *why* your savings account accrues interest over time; by having money sitting in your bank account, you are effectively lending your bank money that your bank can now invest in making profit for itself.

Now, don't run and take your money out of the bank! Those interest payments you receive from your bank are a good thing. But you may wish to consider shopping around for the bank or credit union in your area that offers you the best interest rate payments on that money, or the one whose investments are most in line with your ethics and values.

Either way, now that you know that banks profit off of the money in your account, you understand why your own bank or credit union may have more incentive to offer you a better financing deal than a stranger who doesn't get to invest the money in your bank account, but only the money it can *extract* from your bank account.

And now you know that, in some cases, you can win the credit game by securing funding from your bank or credit union in advance instead of applying through multiple companies for financing.

ASKING THE RIGHT QUESTIONS

You can save yourself from a lot of hard inquiries if you ask the right questions when seeking a loan or a credit line. For example, would you have known before reading this book to look for lenders that don't send hard inquiries to credit bureaus at all, like Credit Builder Card or Self Lender? Would you have known that there was a way you could compare deals across multiple car dealerships with just one hard inquiry on your credit file?

When seeking a new loan or credit card, you can ask questions like:

- Will there be a hard inquiry on my account because of this? Will there be more than one?
- How can we minimize the number of hard inquiries on my account? Lenders and credit card companies just want to get

paid, so they may be able to offer ways to get the same amount of financing with fewer hard inquiries.

- What do you think are the best terms you can offer me? If companies know you will only put in a serious application with the company that offers you the best terms, they will probably be happy to tell you about the best deals they have to offer you to try to coax you into applying with them.

With these tools under your belt, you can optimize your credit history and make the most of every dollar you earn to invest in your future.

CHAPTER 8
GETTING TO "PAID AS AGREED"

"PAID AS AGREED" is the touchdown of the credit world. It is the best possible payment status that you want all of your accounts to show every single month.

The easiest way to do that is to pay all your bills in full and on time. But we all know that isn't always possible. Surprise expenses and shortfalls happen. In some cases, creditors can even fail to notify us that we owe them money while marking us down as non-paying. As long as you are meeting the monthly minimum required payment on all accounts you are paying as agreed, but be careful on accruing interest.

The good news is, it is possible to get your account to "paid as agreed" even long after the original due date has passed. Like the other matters discussed in this book you just have to know *how*.

Some creditors and even debt collectors will change the status of a long past-due account to "paid as agreed" in exchange for full payment. This is the incentive they hold out to you to pay them. You may already have a derogatory mark on your credit report because your bill to them is overdue, but you can have that negative mark erased as though it never happened if you pay the bill now.

However, not all creditors do this automatically. This means that you will want to reach a clear understanding with your creditor that your account status will be changed to "paid as agreed" when you have paid off your balance. This is the only way to ensure that this loss on your scorecard has the best chance of being removed.

So how do you reach such an agreement?

GET IT IN WRITING

Any agreement you reach with *anyone* in your life involving finances should be documented in writing. This allows a court to see clear physical evidence that both parties agreed to these terms, and that you are owed what you were promised for completing your side of the deal.

It is also a good idea to communicate with anyone you might have a complaint with in life such as an employer, doctor, or family member in writing so that there is physical evidence of any problem they have caused you, and of the fact that you let them know about this problem and asked them to help you solve it at the time. That has nothing to do with credit—it's just good to know.

If things go poorly, being able to present a written, signed and time stamped document showing what happened and how both parties agreed to solve the situation is the best way to ensure that justice is done. Any verbal agreement, such as an agreement made via phone call or in-person conversation, is harder to enforce in court since the different parties can give different accounts of what happened. Getting something in writing leaves no doubt.

In the modern world, the easiest way to get an agreement in writing is via email. Email has the added bonus of recording not only the contents of your conversation, but the exact time and date at which the conversation took place and the exact email address of the person you are having the conversation with. That makes it easy to prove who said what and when.

When having a conversation with a creditor about paying a bill where late payment or nonpayment has harmed your credit score, ask for an email or letter stating in writing that they will report the account status to the credit bureaus as "paid as agreed" upon receipt of the payment. If they refuse, you will have less to gain by paying them— and they know that.

During this conversation, you will also want to ask for the best email address to send an email to yourself if the requested email does not show up in your inbox. It is easiest to write an email in reply to an email you've already received, after all, so this will help you make it easier for the creditor to write you this email if they have trouble.

How might you go about asking for something like this? Below I'll share phone and email scripts you can use to help get all of your accounts to "paid as agreed."

PHONE SCRIPT

Many creditors and debt collectors will contact you via phone call, or ask you to call their number as their first line of communication. This is because it's harder to ignore a phone call than an email, and people are more likely to reach a decision to pay if they are encouraged to do so in real-time. Here is a phone script to use when speaking with a creditor or debt collector about getting your account to "paid as agreed."

HOW TO NEGOTIATE WITH BILL COLLECTORS

Remember, you will want to check how close your debt is to expiring under the seven-year statutory limit before contacting any creditor. When you contact them to pay, the clock will reset to "zero" and the derogatory mark will now remain on your credit report for seven years from the date you contact them. So if the bill is already five or six years old, you may not wish to re-start this clock.

For debts which are less than five years old, you may wish to expedite a faster removal from your credit report. In the event that you choose to contact a creditor to arrange this, here are instructions you can use to improve the results of your conversations with this creditor.

Always ask and record who you are talking to. Under the Fair Debt

Collection Practices Act, collectors must identify themselves and the company they work for. If a debt collector or other creditor volunteers this information; write it down. If they don't, ask for the information and then write it down.

Write down the exact date and time of your phone conversation, and its contents. This information may help you later if a dispute arises. If helpful, you may wish to email this information to yourself so that there will be a record on your email server.

"What is your name and the company you work for?"

Immediately write this information down, alongside the date and time of the conversation, when you receive it. You will want to take notes on everything the creditor says during your conversation, ideally writing or typing these notes as you are speaking to them.

Next, tell the creditor your situation.

"I am in a difficult financial position and am behind on my payments. My account number is ____. I'd like to catch up. What kind of payment plan can we arrange?"

You *don't* have to agree to what the creditor proposes. Instead, listen to see what they offer, and see if it is something you can afford. Never agree to borrow money from others, refinance your home, or put debt in a credit card to pay a debt.

If there is no way you can afford to pay under the terms the creditor requests, you may wish to work with a debt settlement lawyer or other financial expert to pursue a more favorable arrangement. If the creditor suggests that you pay more than you can afford, tell them the amount that you have in your budget to pay them.

"I am currently working with a professional with my financial situation. I can pay your company_____ per month for the next _____ months."

Creditors will want to obtain as much payment from you as they can. But if they think the alternative is receiving nothing, they may agree to a more modest payment plan, or even to accept less than the full amount of the debt.

If they offer to accept less than the full amount of the debt or you intend to ask for this, make sure to stipulate that you will need the creditor to agree in writing to report your status as "BIF"—"Balance in Full"—to the credit bureaus. This status looks much better to bureaus than "SIF," which stands for "Settled in Full."

"Once I've made the payments we've agreed upon, we agree that any derogatory information about this account will be removed from my credit report, and my status will be reported to all three credit bureaus as Balance in Full."

Ask what the best email address is to contact the company for a written agreement to report you as BIF once you have paid them the agreed-upon amount.

Once you have obtained an email address or snail mail address, send a confirmation letter to confirm in writing what was discussed today. The notes you have been taking in your phone call log will come in handy for this purpose.

If you send a snail mail letter, keep a copy of the letter and a record of the date and time at which you sent it.

"Thank you <name of collector> of <name of their company>, for working with me.

We agree that I will make monthly payments of _____ beginning on <date> for a total payoff amount of $_____. In return, my status will be reported to all three credit bureaus as "Balance in Full." This letter is to confirm the conclusions of our phone conversation from <date and time of conversation>.

Since we have now reached an agreement, please remove me from your call list. For our mutual protection, we should communicate in writing only from this point on. I do not want you to call me again.

Thank you again for understanding my situation. I am glad we could reach a mutually agreeable arrangement."

If you cannot reach an arrangement that you can afford or which you wish to enter into with the debt collector, tell them you do not wish to pay this debt. This may result in the debt remaining on your credit report for another seven years, but you can stop harassment from debt collectors in this way. If they contact you again after you've told them you do not wish to pay, they've likely violated a law.

Here is a script you can use when requesting no further contacts:

"Please give me the address or email address to which I should send a refusal to pay and cease and desist letter in accordance with the law. I am revoking permission for you to call me at any phone number. I am making a written record of this revocation of permission."

NEGOTIATING TO PAY LESS

It is sometimes possible to negotiate with creditors to pay less than the full amount they are asking for while still getting to "paid as agreed" status. However, this must be done within a certain time window, and requires the use of very specific wording and some knowledge of the collections industry to be successful.

Because the way to do this successfully is not simple, may be different depending on the type of creditor, and is not possible for accounts whose time window has passed, I have not attempted to address every possible situation that may arise here. However, I do offer assistance with these techniques as part of my Major League Credit Repair services.

I also offer you the following template for a letter (not a phone call —you need this in writing!) for your use if you wish to try this technique without assistance:

To Whom It May Concern:

On (Date), I received a copy of my credit report from (Credit Bureau Name). That report lists my payments to you as being 'delinquent.'

My financial problems are now behind me and I am in a position to pay off this debt. I can pay a lump sum amount of $_____ or I can pay installments in the amount of $_____ per month for _____ months if you will agree to one of the following:

( ) If I make a lump sum payment, you will agree to remove all negative information from my credit file associated with the debt.

( ) If I agree to pay off the debt in monthly installments, you agree to 're-age' my account - making the current month the first repayment month and showing no late payments as long as I make the agreed upon monthly payments.

If this offer is acceptable to you, please check and initial one of the above choices, sign your acceptance below and return this letter to me in the enclosed envelope.

Thank you for your time and assistance.

Sincerely yours,

Unfortunately, this script may have lower chances of success if used without assistance. It may not be possible to negotiate at all if the time window for doing so on a specific debt has passed, and as with all negotiations, there is an art to determining what offer will be appealing enough to be accepted while still being optimally beneficial to you. This is where an experienced expert's eye can be useful.

My Major League Credit Repair services also offer assistance with legally complex situations like bankruptcy, identity theft, and other unfortunate circumstances that may occur when bills go unpaid. We have experts including experienced attorneys who are available free of charge to those who have documentation proving negligence or inaccurate reporting of a debt.

I have not attempted to advise about these in this book because they happen to few people and mistakes made in dealing with them can be costly, but if you are experiencing such a situation, don't hesitate to reach out to my Major League Credit Repair company for help!

CHAPTER 9
DISPUTING ERRORS

IN ADDITION to navigating the credit game to win as much as possible, unfortunately, we have to worry about errors on our scorecard. Whether because of bureaucratic errors or identity theft, we can end up with charges and derogatory marks on our credit report for purchases we never made or bills we've already paid.

This is one reason why it's so important to monitor your credit report and credit score: you can do everything right, and it is still possible that your score will take a hit which you will need to work to resolve.

Credit report errors happen often in two basic ways. It's worth taking the time to discuss both of them so that you will be well-equipped to prevent and address them.

IDENTITY THEFT

Identity theft is an increasingly serious problem in the digital age. More and more online transactions means it's easier than ever before for impersonators to steal your credit or identity information, and use that information to make purchases or open lines of credit in your name.

Since these imposters will not take hits to their own credit score as a result of nonpayment, they will have no incentive to pay the bills they rack up while using your identity. You can then be unpleasantly surprised with negative marks on your credit score or calls from creditors and debt collectors.

Avoiding identity theft means keeping your information safe. That means not giving information that can be used to open accounts in your name to people you don't know well (or to *anybody* else if you can help it), and being cautious when transmitting such data on the Internet.

Pieces of information that can potentially be used by a stranger to open a credit account in your name include:

- Your full legal name
- Your date of birth
- Your phone number
- Your Social Security Number
- Any information about your past or current street addresses
- Any information about your past or current loan history
- Information about your pets, your mother's maiden name, or other questions that may be used as security questions for your online accounts.

Because of these risks, be cautious of any individual or website that asks for such information. Is it a trusted website that you are engaging with for purposes of conducting business, such as the website of a credit bureau or your existing bank or creditor?

The same goes for unsolicited phone calls. Never give any of this information on the phone to a stranger who calls your telephone. If someone calls claiming to be from a company you do business with and asks for this information, it's a good idea to hang up and call the trusted phone number you have for that company to ask whether the call was legitimate. In this way you may protect not only yourself, but also protect others by helping the company become aware of scammers who are impersonating them.

Some organizations which are impersonated by scammers hoping to extract money or information that can be used to steal your identity include:

- The IRS. (Generally, the IRS will never call you and demand money or your Social Security number. They communicate almost exclusively through postal mail.)
- Credit card companies. (Generally these will not make unsolicited phone calls; you will be the one calling them if you are applying, and they will usually communicate any problems with your account via postal mail or through an online account portal with a secure, verified website you have signed up with.)
- Other government agencies. Some scammers have even called immigrants falsely posing as the government of their home country in an effort to extract money and identity information from them. Talk about underhanded!

The Internet is another important frontier for safety. Most legitimate companies have online portals which may ask for some of the above information to verify it's really you. This is done in order to *prevent* identity theft. But be wary of any website which asks for the information above which you are *not* already doing business with.

The same rules about phone calls apply to unsolicited emails you receive. Legitimate companies generally will not request information such as your Social Security number via email. Some scammers and identity thieves may also send emails posing as an organization you do business with, containing a link to a website that asks you for this information.

If you are not completely positive that an email came from the company you do business with, it's a good idea to call the company and check. Any information a company is asking you to enter into a web form or email, it can usually collect more securely over the phone. You can ask to give them your information via phone instead of through the Internet by calling the business's trusted phone number.

Look the number up yourself from a reliable independent source instead of calling the number listed in a suspicious email or unsolicited phone message to make sure you are getting through to the real organization and not a scammer posing as them.

Unfamiliar websites should never ask for your Social Security number, and "harmless" questions in online quizzes about matters like your childhood pet or the street you grew up on can sometimes be masks for the collection of data to be used in identity theft.

If a website asks for any of this information and you are not sure about its security, it is a good idea to use a search engine to research the organization for any reports of scams, or to call the organization on the phone if you know the company is legit but are not sure that this website is secure.

Arguably one of the most important ways to prevent identity theft in the modern era is simply to avoid transmitting data over public wifi networks.

These are the kinds of networks you run into at airports, coffee shops, and other public spaces. They are accessed by many people, and may appear free to access without the necessity for a password.

The problem is, this freedom of access makes it easier for hackers to steal your data from them. Hackers may even set up their own wireless networks in public spaces which *look* like they are being offered by a local organization, but which may actually be run by an individual who harvests all the data transmitted over the network.

One of the best identity defenses out there is a VPN—a virtual private network which masks and encrypts your data. These are often very affordable, and are growing increasingly popular as they offer many benefits including enhanced privacy and security, and other features.

Another useful tool is your phone's wifi hotspot. A growing number of smartphones have the ability to create their own wireless Internet connection which your computer can use anywhere your phone is present. These wifi hotspots have the same level of security as your cell phone data network, making them safer to use to transmit sensitive data than unsecured networks in public spaces.

Using a phone's wifi hotspot to surf the Internet may eat into your phone's data plan, but when you must transmit data that could be used to commit identity theft in a public place, it's worth the cost in data.

SIMILAR NAME ERRORS

Another common cause of credit report errors is quite simply when two people have similar names. This is more likely when you have a Junior and a Senior in the same family who have the same first and last name, or when you have a very common name like John Smith. In these cases, credit bureaus and creditors alike may get confused and put charges or late payments on the wrong John Smith's account.

Unfortunately this is difficult to avoid, since you don't generally choose your own name at birth. But it may be a factor to consider when considering whether to give a baby exactly the same first and last name as another living person. Most John Smiths will be fortunate enough to get through life without such an error, but if it does happen it can be a real headache to resolve.

DISPUTING ERRORS

If you notice an error on a bill or on your credit report, you will have to dispute it. Today, most companies, including credit bureaus, have a simple button you can press to report a fraudulent charge or dispute an item on your credit report. This is a good first step. However, unfortunately this does not always solve the problem.

When a company rejects your claim of a fraudulent charge or an error on your credit report, you will likely have to resort to sending a lengthy campaign of letters using specific language and dispute tactics to try to get the item removed.

You send letters because you want all of this in writing so that the courts can see that this is a mistake and you have been trying to resolve it; you use specific credit compliance language so that the e-Oscar system can work to your benefit and creditors you are disputing will know that you are aware of the legal remedies available to you if they genuinely have made a mistake and they fail to correct it. Knowing that you are aware that you may be able to sue them over such a mistake gives them incentive to investigate and correct the error.

I am including below a sample of a dispute letter you may wish to send to a credit bureau if you discover an error on your report and the initial dispute you file through their "dispute" function is rejected.

> To Whom It May Concern:
>
> I received a copy of my credit report and found the following item(s) to be errors.
>
> {dispute_item_and_explanation}
>
> By the provisions of the Fair Credit Reporting Act, I demand that these items be investigated and removed from my report. It is my understanding that you will re-check these items with the creditor who has posted them. Please remove any information that the creditor cannot verify. I understand that under 15 U.S.C. Sec. 1681i(a), you must complete this reinvestigation within 30 days of receipt of this letter.
>
> Sincerely yours,

If you do not receive a satisfactory response within 60 days of sending this letter, here is another letter you can send to escalate the situation:

> To Whom It May Concern,
>
> This letter is a formal complaint that you are reporting inaccurate and incomplete credit information.
>
> I am distressed that you have included the information below in my credit profile and that you have failed to maintain reasonable procedures in your operations to assure maximum possible accuracy in the credit reports you publish. Credit reporting laws ensure that bureaus report only 100% accurate credit information.
>
> Every step must be taken to assure the information reported is

completely accurate and correct. The following information, therefore, needs to be re-investigated. I respectfully request to be provided proof of this alleged item, specifically the contract, note or other instrument bearing my signature.

{dispute_item_and_explanation}

Failing that, the item must be deleted from the report as soon as possible. The listed item is entirely inaccurate and incomplete, and as such represents a very serious error in your reporting. Please delete this misleading information and supply a corrected credit profile to all creditors who have received a copy within the last six months, or the last two years for employment purposes.

Additionally, please provide the name, address, and telephone number of each credit grantor or other subscribers.

Under federal law, you have thirty (30) days to complete your re-investigation. Be advised that the description of the procedure used to determine the accuracy and completeness of the information is hereby requested as well, to be provided within fifteen (15) days of the completion of your re-investigation.

Sincerely yours,

This is just one sample—if they do not respond to this letter favorably, you may need to write a series of letters using escalating legal language to resolve the issue. This is another expert-level matter where specific details about what has happened may affect what language you must use in your letter to be successful.

It may also become necessary to provide the credit bureaus with proof that you have done all that is necessary to address the situation on your end, such as supplying proof that you have filed police reports and complaints to the Federal Trade Commission about the theft of your identity.

Because of the complexity of escalating disputes, I am not including further dispute letter templates here. But I do offer a collection of dispute letter templates for a variety of possible situations, and expert advice to help you determine which one is appropriate for your situation through Major League Credit Repair.

Fixing errors on your credit report can be difficult, and you may feel powerless if your first few attempts to have an error corrected are rejected or ignored. But you are not powerless! As you can tell by the language of the second letter, there are laws in place requiring credit bureaus to do their job, and procedures that they must follow. This is called the Fair Credit Reporting Act.

As with all things in the credit game, all you need to gain a big advantage is knowledge, and the patience and persistence to follow the necessary steps to accomplish your goals.

When you have those two things, you have power.

CHAPTER 10
IMPROVING YOUR EXISTING ACCOUNTS

You may already have credit cards, or you may start to open a new credit card account or two after raising your credit score using the techniques in this book. Either way, one little-known fact is that you can often get better terms on your credit accounts after your credit score goes up, even if you opened the account when your credit was not quite so excellent.

Credit card companies compete for great credit players. That means that if they see that you're an all-star and you express that you're less than thrilled with the terms of your current account with them, they will often offer you better terms in an attempt to keep you on their team.

In the eyes of credit card companies, getting paid a low interest rate by someone who always pays their bills on time and who may be on their way to being a big spender is better than getting paid no interest because you left their company and accepted a better offer.

You can ask for improvements to your credit card accounts like:

- A lower interest rate.
- A higher credit limit.

Remember, you don't want to get a higher credit limit because you want to be able to charge $10,000 on your credit card—that would harm your credit! You want to get a higher limit so that you can have more credit available to you in case an emergency leaves you with no other way to pay for things, and so that you can charge more on your account without going over the 10% limit for ideal credit usage that makes your score look great. 30% is the absolute max in case you have to tend to a larger purchase or emergency.

You might get a $10,000 credit limit and never charge more than $1,000 at once on that card. That's actually ideal. But because your credit limit is so high, you can charge a whole $1,000 on there without taking a big hit to your credit score due to high utilization, and you have a whole $10,000 in credit to fall back on if something really bad happens and there's just no other way to put food on the table for a few months.

And once you've got a great interest rate on that card, anything you charge on it will cost you much less than it would have cost to pay for with a payday loan or a higher-interest card.

Once your credit score has gone up, making you a more desirable player than you were before, here are some telephone scripts you can use to call your credit card company and ask for better terms:

LOWER INTEREST RATE TELEPHONE SCRIPT

YOU: Hello, I'd like to lower the APR on my credit card, please.

CREDIT CARD REP: May I ask why?

YOU: I've been a loyal customer to you for X years. Also, I've paid my bill in full and on time for the past few months/years. I know a few other credit cards offering better rates than what I'm getting right now, and I'd hate for this interest rate to drive me away from your service. What can you do for me?

CREDIT CARD REP: Hmm. Let me check...Ms. Patrick, I just discovered that I am able to lower your rate from 15% to 12%. Will this work?

HIGHER CREDIT LIMIT TELEPHONE SCRIPT

YOU: Hello, I'd like to increase the limit on my credit card, please.

CREDIT CARD REP: May I ask why?

YOU: I've been a loyal customer to you for X years. Also, I've paid my bill in full and on time for the past few months/years. I've been offered cards with higher limits by some of your competitors, and I would hate for a low credit limit to drive me away from your service.

CREDIT CARD REP: Hmm. Let me check…Ms. Patrick, I just discovered that I am able to lower your rate from $5,000 to $10,000. Will this work?

It's common that during uncertain economic times, credit card companies may automatically lower the credit card limits of many users. The companies may become concerned about losing money if many users start using them as an emergency fund and can't pay them back.

This happened at the start of the COVID-19 pandemic, when many credit card companies became concerned that large numbers of their customers may soon face job loss or huge medical bills. To reduce the risk to the company, these credit card companies cut many users' credit limits.

When this happens, it is not because the cardholder has done something wrong—it is a systemic measure taken to reduce risk to the company. The company will usually also offer to increase the users' credit limits again once the crisis has passed and the economy is looking up. If your credit limit was cut by your credit card company in 2020 and you have been faithfully paying your bills for the last few months or years, there is a good chance you can now get your credit limit raised back up to its former glory or beyond with a phone call.

IMPROVING LOANS AND MORTGAGES

Other types of credit lines, such as loans and mortgages, can also be improved from their original terms as you learn more about credit and become more creditworthy. These changes tend to be very complex and require a lot of work, however, since the amounts of these loans are often very large.

A clever refinancing may save your family $100,000 or more if done properly, but this can usually only be done with the help of an expert. When taking an interest in refinancing or getting a loan modification, it is important to have a trusted expert on your side. Some companies can offer refinancing deals and loan modifications that sound great in the advertisement, but which contain hidden details in the fine print that can leave you worse off than you were before in the interest of profiting the company.

When seeking an expert to help you with a refinancing or loan modification, look for an expert who is trusted by people you trust and who has reason to have your best interest in mind. You may be able to accomplish something extraordinary—but like all of life's greatest achievements, you probably will not be able to succeed alone.

CHAPTER 11
INTRODUCTION TO BUSINESS CREDIT

YOU NOW KNOW the most fundamental principles of personal credit. This powerful knowledge will help you to build generational wealth and avoid the traps of permanent debt and poverty that too many people fall into. There is still more to learn—now that you know how powerful these principles are, you may desire to study some of the complex topics mentioned here and become a credit educator or financial professional yourself someday.

But believe it or not, we've barely scratched the surface of how credit determines who becomes wealthy and who stays poor.

I mentioned that credit can be used to obtain business loans a few times throughout this book. Business loans and business credit cards carry several wealth-building advantages over personal loans and personal credit cards. This is because business loans and business credit are the real heavy lifters in our economy.

For those who know how, tens or hundreds of thousands of dollars in capital to start a business or invest in real estate can be acquired with no money out-of-pocket and little risk to one's personal and family finances. If you also acquire the business know how to multiply that money—something that is totally achievable without going to business school—you can see how you can rapidly build hundreds or millions of dollars for your family and community.

This process begins with building great personal credit. Just like with personal credit, business creditors and lenders will look at your payment history to determine how much they can safely lend you, at what interest rate, and what kinds of collateral in terms of assets they may require you to put on the line in order to approve your loan. When you are first starting out securing business credit, your personal credit score can be used to determine these factors. This can also be done separate from your personal credit by obtaining credit using your business Employer Identification Number also known as an EIN.

Once you have established the basic forms of business credit, you will want to focus on developing positive payment history for your business. Your business has a separate credit score from your personal credit, and that is how you build it.

This is an incredibly powerful tool. It means that, for example, if your business fails due to unforeseen circumstances, its unpaid bills may not affect your personal credit and your personal ability to get home loans, low interest rates, etc. at all. This powerful separation can also work in reverse: if a personal disaster means that you have to declare personal bankruptcy, your business may still be able to obtain big loans and low interest rates as long as your business has been paying its bills.

Separating your business from your personal credit and finances will require incorporating your business as a separate legal entity from you as an individual. Your business will then receive an Employer Identification Number—the business equivalent of a Social Security Number—and will file separate taxes for you as an individual.

This may sound like a hassle, but it is not as intimidating as it sounds. Anyone can incorporate an LLC and begin applying for business credit cards to begin building business credit.

It's important to incorporate your business for other reasons beyond your business credit score. Corporations may sometimes be eligible for special tax breaks, grants, and other programs that individuals cannot qualify for.

Incorporating limits not only your financial liability for the actions of your business, but also the legal liability. If your business is sued or fined, your personal finances may be protected from the fines or the lawsuit if your business is a separate incorporated entity and you were not personally responsible for any wrongdoing.

All of these are reasons to incorporate your business—a move which will also make your business eligible for the tremendous power of business credit.

The majority of you reading this book probably don't yet own a corporation. You may not be ready to start one, either, if your personal credit score is not yet great and might not get you great rates on business credit cards and business loans.

Major League Credit has a proven system that can help you start or grow your business by establishing business credit and accessing various types of loans and capital. Our business credit-building system also comes with six months of personal credit repair! We want to make it easy for you to kill two birds with one stone, since both processes do take time.

So take some time to nurture your credit, and then keep an eye out for my next book. This book will cover the basics of business credit in the same way I've covered the basics of personal credit here, and will detail some of the things that Major League Credit's business credit experts can help you with.

I wish you wealth and happiness in the years to come. You deserve it.

RESOURCES

- *Welcome to Major League Credit & Lending.* https://majorleaguecr.com/
- *Book a Free Consultation with Major League Credit & Lending.* Calendly. https://calendly.com/majorleaguecreditrepair
- SelfLender. *Welcome to Self Lender.* https://self.inc/refer/16576650
- RentReporters. *Report rent payments, Build your credit score.* (2022, June 8). https://prf.hn/l/6bW31aO
- Credit Builder Card. *It's time to Build your credit.* https://www.creditbuildercard.com/majorleaguecreditrepair.html
- Kikoff Credit Builder | Build Credit Safely & Responsibly. *Build credit with Kikoff.* https://kikoff.com/
- Annual Credit Report.com - Home Page. https://www.annualcreditreport.com/index.action
- SmartCredit. *Credit scores and reports with monitoring.* http://www.smartcredit.com/majorleaguecreditrepair
- IdentityIQ. *3 credit scores, Daily Credit Monitoring & Alerts.* https://www.identityiq.com/get-all-your-reports-now.aspx?offercode=431131QO

- Experian.com. Do more with your FICO® score. all free. https://www.experian.com. 1-888-397-3742
- Equifax.com. Credit Bureau: Check your credit report & credit score. https://www.equifax.com. 1-800-525-6285
- Transunion.com. Credit scores, Credit Reports & Credit Check. https://www.transunion.com. 1-800-680-7289.
- Utica University. Identity Theft Victims' Resources. Resources - identity crimes - center for identity management and information protection (CIMIP) - Utica University. https://www.utica.edu/academic/institutes/cimip/idcrimes/resources.cfm
- *Fair credit reporting act.* (2020, March 4). Federal Trade Commission. Retrieved August 1, 2022, from https://www.ftc.gov/legal-library/browse/statutes/fair-credit-reporting-act
- *Fair debt collection practices act.* (2016, March 23). Federal Trade Commission. Retrieved August 1, 2022, from https://www.ftc.gov/legal-library/browse/rules/fair-debt-collection-practices-act-text
- *Major League Credit Repair.* Facebook. https://www.facebook.com/majorleaguecreditrepair
- *Major League Credit Repair.* Instagram. (@majorleaguecredit) • instagram photos and videos. https://www.instagram.com/majorleaguecredit

ABOUT THE AUTHOR

Chevon K. Patrick is a credit educator, and founder and President of Major League Credit Repair, LLC. She established Major League Credit Repair after realizing how much she and her peers had not been taught about credit and finance in school or life. After discovering that good credit is the key to financial literacy, and to multiplying wealth using other people's money, Chevon set out to provide education and expert assistance to others like herself.

Chevon has a particular passion for serving, educating, and investing in Black communities and Black business owners. She has seen how historical injustice and lack of financial education opportunities too often creates a cycle of poverty.

Chevon is also a mother, a cancer survivor, a student, and a believer in spiritual healing. She currently lives with her youngest son Kaelon while admiring the musical talent and career of her older son, Taejon. She is still, unfortunately, grieving the loss of her youngest daughter, Yevaeh, who was nine. It is her profound hope that the soul as well as the entire body of the Black community can be healed and made whole through God, skillful use of financial education, spiritual guidance and whatever else may be necessary to build overall prosperity.

Website: https://majorleaguecr.com/
Consultations: calendly.com/majorleaguecreditrepair

facebook.com / majorleaguecreditrepair
instagram.com / majorleaguecredit